Mechanics are using a hand pump to transfer 200 litres of 87 octane fuel from a drum to Jabo, Immola, Finland, 28 June 1944. This Focke Wulf Fw 190F-8 belonged to 1./SG 5, which was ex-14.(Jabo)/JG 5. It formed the fighter-bomber element of *Gefechtsverband* Kuhlmey, which was sent to Immola on 22 June and stayed there until 3 August 1944. "Black 6" was usually flown by *Oblt.* Walter Schneller. (SA-kuva)

# LUFTWAFFE AT WAR

# Luftwaffe over Finland

# Kari Stenman
and
Kalevi Keskinen

Greenhill Books
LONDON

Stackpole Books
PENNSYLVANIA

Greenhill Books

*Luftwaffe Over Finland* first published 2001 by Greenhill Books, Lionel Leventhal Limited, Park House, 1 Russell Gardens, London NW11 9NN
www.greenhillbooks.com
and
Stackpole Books, 5067 Ritter Road, Mechanicsburg, PA 17055, USA

*British Library Cataloguing in Publication Data:*
Stenman, Kari
The Luftwaffe over Finland. – (Luftwaffe at war; 18)
1. Germany. Luftwaffe – History – World War, 1939–1945
2. World War, 1939-1945 – Finland. 3. World War, 1939–1945 – Aerial operations, German
I. Title
940.5'44'943

ISBN 1-85367-469-9

*Library of Congress Cataloging-in-Publication Data available.*

Designed by DAG Publications Ltd
Design by David Gibbons
Layout by Anthony A. Evans
Edited by Andy Oppenheimer
Printed in Singapore

# LUFTWAFFE OVER FINLAND

## GENERAL MILITARY OPERATIONS ON THE NORTHERN FRONT

Germany started the World War II by attacking Poland on 1 September 1939. According to the preferential agreement between Germany and the Soviet Union – the Nazi-Soviet Pact of August 1939 – the former occupied the western part, and the latter, the eastern part of Poland. Backed by that same pact, Soviet Union attacked Finland on 30 November 1939, but Finland fought back and retained its independence in a peace treaty signed on 13 March 1940, which ended the winter war. To improve its strategic positions in Europe, Germany invaded Denmark and southern Norway on 9 April 1940, and regained control over the whole of Norway by mid-June 1940. After taking Holland, Belgium, and France in May and June 1940, only Britain was left unconquered. Germany fought the Battle of Britain and lost. It then turned to the east.

For its forthcoming eastern campaign Germany reconditioned and expanded several airbases and ports in northern Norway and obtained right of way for troops to pass through neutral Sweden and Finland. By diplomacy or pressure, Germany won over all the Soviet Union's western neighbours, from the Arctic Sea to the Black Sea. Operation Barbarossa, the German invasion of Russia, was launched on 22 June 1941.

The German army group *Nord* advanced towards Leningrad through the Baltic countries, which had been annexed by the Soviet Union a year earlier, arriving at the Gulf of Finland in August 1941. It encircled Leningrad the following month, but never reached the city. The operation was supported by *Luftflotte* 1.

Further north on the eastern front, the Finns conquered the Karelian Isthmus in two months and encircled Leningrad from the north by September 1941. A month later the Finnish troops had occupied the isthmus of Olonets and advanced to the isthmus of Maaselkä, between Lake Onega and the White Sea.

At the Arctic Sea the German army, AOK *Norwegen*, was unable to come any closer than 50 kilometres from Murmansk or the White Sea. The front ran through the wilderness a few tens of kilometres west of the Murmansk railway to the isthmus of Maaselkä.

A protracted stalemate began in autumn 1941 and lasted for almost three years. The Finns were responsible for the front up to the Oulu-Uhtua line and the Germans north of it up to the Arctic Sea.

In June 1944 the Soviet Union attacked on the Karelian Isthmus and Olonets. The Finns halted all Russian advances in two months and on 4 September 1944 disengaged from the war by calling a truce with the Soviet Union. The truce stipulated the removal of German troops from northern parts of Finland. After declaring war on Germany, the Finns had practically driven out the German troops by November 1944.

In October 1944 the Soviet Union attacked on the Arctic front and within a month had pushed the Germans back from Petsamo and Kirkenes. The German troops in northern Norway then retreated southwards to Lyngen-Narvik, which they held at the time of Germany's capitulation on 8 May 1945.

In Norway and northern Finland *Luftflotte* 5 was in charge of aerial operations. From May 1940 it was commanded by *Generaloberst* Hans-Jürgen Stumpff and from November 1943 by *Generalleutnant* Josef Kammhuber. In October 1944 the remaining northern units were combined as '*Die Deutsche Luftwaffe in Norwegen*' with *Generalleutnant* Ernst-August Roth in command until the end of hostilities.

## MAIN LUFTFLOTTE 5 UNITS

### Fighter Outfits

During the invasion of Norway, II./JG 77 was in charge of fighter operations with Messerschmitt Bf 109E aircraft. At the beginning of 1941 I./JG 77 was re-formed in Norway. When Operation Barbarossa began on 22 June 1941, two out of the four *Staffeln* were deployed to the east, equipped with Bf 109E and Bf 109T aircraft. In September I./JG 77 was divided into *Jagdgruppe Stavanger* in the south and *Jagdstaffel Kirkenes* in the north. In November 1941 the latter was expanded to JGr.z.b.V, which operated four *Staffeln*.

At the very beginning of 1942 *Jagdgeschwader* 5 was formed to take over all fighter operations in *Luftflotte* 5 area. *Jagdgruppe Stavanger* became I./JG 5, which had three *Staffeln* in southern Norway. It was equipped with Bf 109E, F and G plus Focke Wulf Fw 190A fighter aircraft.

II./JG 5 was formed in Kirkenes in March 1942 and its three *Staffeln* were based at Petsamo and Alakurtti. In early November 1943 the *Gruppe* was transferred to *Luftflotte* 1, from where it paid a two-month visit to Alakurtti in early March 1944. The machines were Bf 109E, F and G versions.

At the same time as the formation of II *Gruppe*, III./JG 5 was formed at Trondheim and usually flew from Petsamo with three *Staffeln*. In December 1944 the *Gruppe* moved to southern Norway. The *Geschwader* staff, Stab/JG 5, was linked with this *Gruppe*. III./JG 5 was equipped with Bf 109E, F and G plus Fw 190A and F planes.

IV./JG 5 was formed at Trondheim in June 1942 and the *Gruppe* operated three *Staffeln* for westward defence over central and northern Norway. In October 1944 the unit repelled the Soviet attack in Petsamo sector and flew to southern Norway the following month. Messerschmitt Bf 109E, T, F and G plus Fw 190A and F fighters were in the inventory.

At the beginning of 1943 14.(Jabo)/JG 5 was formed and the *Staffel* flew from Petsamo with Focke Wulf Fw 190A fighter-bombers. In January 1944 the unit was renamed 4./SG 5 and renamed again, as 1./SG 5, in May. The *Staffel* flew Fw 190Fs with *Gefechtsverband* Kuhlmey from mid-June 1944 and left Finland with its *Gruppe* in mid-August 1944.

Parts of ZG 76 were subdued by I./JG 77 in spring 1941. At the beginning of 1942 this heavy fighter *Staffel* became 6.(Z)/JG 5, in March 1942 changing to 10.(Z)/JG 5, and renamed again three months later as 13.(Z)/JG 5. In February 1944 the *Staffel* moved to southern Norway. It was equipped with Messerschmitt Bf 110E, F and G planes and flew mainly from Kirkenes.

### Other Fighter Outfits

Detachments of JG 54 belonging to *Luftflotte* 1 and operating south of Leningrad flew occasionally in Finland. *Kommando* I./JG 54 flew top cover for a German-Italian naval unit with 15 Messerschmitt Bf 109F fighters in Lake Ladoga. It was based at Petäjärvi for three months from early July 1942.

To assist the Finns in repelling the Soviet major attack on the Karelian Isthmus, the main parts of II./JG 54, as part of *Gefechtsverband* Kuhlmey, arrived in mid-June 1944. It consisted of 25 Focke Wulf Fw 190A fighters and was based at Immola for five weeks.

To fight against the Soviet night bombers attacking Helsinki in February 1944, a 12-plane *Staffel* of I./JG 302 from the *Reichsverteidigung* (defence of the *Reich*) was sent to Finland. It operated for three months from Malmi.

### Bomber Units

IV./LG 1 took part in the invasion of Norway and by the beginning of the eastern campaign it was transferred to Kirkenes. Three *Staffeln* equipped with Junkers Ju 87B or R dive bombers also operated from Rovaniemi. The *Gruppe* was re-named I./St.G 5 in January 1942 and the unit was also based at Alakurtti until flying south of Leningrad in January 1943.

In summer 1943 the re-formed I./St.G 5 was equipped with Junkers Ju 87D dive-bombers and was stationed at Nautsi. In the following October, all *Stukageschwadern* became *Schlachtgeschwadern* but kept the numbering. In December 1943 I./SG 5 was transferred to *Luftflotte* 1 and returned to Kemijärvi in March 1944. In May it deployed Fw 190Fs and moved to Pontsalenjoki. The *Gruppe* operated from Utti for a time until flying to Estonia in mid-August 1944.

On 16 June 1944, as part of *Gefechtsverband* Kuhlmey, I./SG 3 arrived at Immola with 25 Ju 87D dive bombers. After good work in repelling the Soviet attack spearheads the *Gruppe* left Finland on 21 July 1944.

NSGr. 8 was formed in Rovaniemi for a night harrassment role in January 1944. It was equipped with Arado Ar 66c biplanes and was based at Pontsalenjoki. In summer 1944 two *Staffeln* converted to Ju 87D aircraft. In October 1944 the *Gruppe* withdrew to Norway.

I./KG 26 participated in the invasion of Norway and was stationed at Trondheim at the beginning of Operation Barbarossa. The *Gruppe* arrived at Kemi in August 1941. Equipped with Heinkel He 111Hs in three *Staffeln*, from October 1941 it also flew from Banak and Petsamo. During spring 1942 the *Gruppe* converted to He 111H torpedo bombers, which operated against Allied shipping until November 1942, when it flew to the Mediterranean.

III./KG 26 equipped with Junkers Ju 88A torpedo bombers was transferred to Banak in July 1942 to fight the Allied ship convoys. The convoys were brought to a halt in November 1942 and the *Gruppe* flew to the Mediterranean to counter the Allied invasion in North Africa.

I./KG 30 arrived at Banak in August 1941 with Junkers Ju 88A bombers. Flying from Kemi and Petsamo, it dwindled to a *Staffel* size and in May 1942 returned to Banak, fully equipped with Ju 88A torpedo bombers. Fighting against Allied shipping in the North Atlantic and Arctic Sea, it left in July 1943 as the last bomber outfit in *Luftflotte* 5 area.

One *Staffel* of II./KG 30 was based at Kirkenes at the start of hostilities and in August 1941 the whole *Gruppe* flew to southern Norway. With the Allied convoys it returned to Banak in April 1942, and left for the Mediterranean in November 1942. During that period it had been equipped with Ju 88A bombers.

III./KG 30 was transferred to the north from March 1942 against Allied shipping. The *Gruppe* was based at Bardufoss, Nautsi and Banak. In November 1942 it left for southern Europe.

### Reconnaissance Units
Throughout the war the close-range reconnaissance of the Arctic Sea front was the responsibility of 1./(H)/Aufkl.Gr. 32, which was based at Kemijärvi at the beginning of the eastern campaign. Other bases used were Petsamo and Alakurtti. The *Staffel* was equipped with Henschel Hs 126B, Focke Wulf Fw 189A and Messerschmitt Bf 109G aircraft. In December 1944 the outfit flew to Norway as the last German flying unit in Finland.

In June 1941 the long-range reconnaissance unit 1.(F)/Aufkl.Gr. 124 moved to its main base at Kirkenes. In October 1944 the *Staffel* left for Banak. Its equipment consisted mostly of Junkers Ju 88A and D aircraft, as well as Dornier Do 215B, Messerschmitt Bf 109G and Junkers Ju 188F planes.

In July 1941 another long-range reconnaissance *Staffel*, 1.(F)/Aufkl.Gr. 22, arrived at Kirkenes. It was based at Banak from March 1942 until December 1944, when it flew to Germany. It was equipped with Junkers Ju 88A and D, plus Ju 188D versions.

### Other Units
When Operation Barbarossa began in June 1941, coastal patrol unit 1./Kü.Fl.Gr. 406 was equipped with Heinkel He 115C seaplanes. It flew mainly from Tromsö and Nordreisa and was disbanded in October 1944.

In July 1943 SAGr. 130 was formed from sections of Kü.Fl.Gr. 406, 706 and 906. The *Gruppe* was based at Billefjord and flew Blohm und Voss Bv 138C flying boats for the remainder of the war.

In Finland aircraft of several transport units flew, of which KGr.z.b.V 108 took part in the invasion of Norway in April 1940 and stayed there. It was equipped with Junkers Ju 52 land or seaplanes. In May 1943 the unit was renamed TGr. 20 for the remainder of the war.

## FIGHTER ACES IN THE NORTH

### Oberfeldwebel Heinrich Bartels
Bartels was born on 13 July 1918 in Linz, Austria. He joined 8./JG 5 in April 1942 and received the *Ritterkreuz* (Knight's Cross) on 13 November 1942 for 45 kills. In summer 1943 he was transferred to IV./JG 27 in the Mediterranean. On 23 December 1944 he went missing in action following combat with Thunderbolts. His tally stood then at 99 victories, 47 of which was with JG 5.

### Oberfeldwebel Alfred Brunner
Brunner was born on 17 July 1918 at Dörtel in Württenberg. He joined 6./JG 5 in April 1942. On 7 May 1943 his Bf 109G-2 (WNr 14802) was shot down by 2 GIAP Airacobras; he bailed out too low and was killed. On 3 July 1943 he received the *Ritterkreuz* posthumously for 53 aerial victories.

### Major Horst Carganico
Carganico was born on 27 September 1917 in Breslau. At the beginning of Operation Barbarossa he was commanding 1./JG 77, which was operating at the Arctic Sea. On 25 September 1941 he received the *Ritterkreuz* for 25 kills. When 6./JG 5 was formed in March 1942, he took over command of it. Next month he was made *Kommandeur* of II./JG 5. In March 1944 he became *Kommandeur* of I./JG 5, which had been transferred to the defence of Germany. On 27 May 1944 he was killed in his Bf 109G after being hit by return fire from US bombers. His tally came to 60, all but four being with JG 5 or its predecessors.

### Hauptmann Hugo Dahmer
Dahmer was born on 7 May 1918 in Koblenz. In spring 1940 he joined 6./JG 26. In spring 1941 he was posted to 1./JG 77, joining Operation Barbarossa. On 1 August 1941 he became the first *Rittekreuz* holder in the north with 22 kills. From the founding of 6./JG 5 in March 1942, he flew with this unit until being posted back to 6./JG 26 in late 1942. As a member of III./JG 2 he was seriously wounded on 10 October 1943 and no longer flew combat missions. His total score stood at 57 victories, 25 with JG 5 and its predecessors.

### Leutnant Hans Döbrich
Döbrich was born on 24 March 1916 in Sonnenberg, Thüringen. He flew with 6./JG 5, which was established in March 1942. On 16 July 1943 his Bf 109G-6 (WNr 20088) was shot down by 20 IAP Yak-1s. Although rescued, he was badly wounded and did not return to combat missions. On 19 September 1943 he was awarded the *Ritterkreuz* for 65 aerial victories.

### Hauptmann Franz Dörr
Dörr was born on 10 February 1913 in Mannheim. Originally a reconnaissance pilot, he was retrained to fighter-pilot status and joined 7./JG 5 in March 1942. In September 1943 he took over 7./JG 5 after Weissenberger. On 19 August 1944 he received the *Ritterkreuz* for 95 aerial victories. In May 1944 he

became the last *Kommandeur* of III./JG 5. He claimed 128 kills, all but six with JG 5 and a maximum of 12 on 27 June 1944. He died on 17 October 1972.

### Major Heinrich Ehrler

Ehrler was born on 14 September 1917 in Oberballach in Baden. He became a fighter pilot in 1940 and flew with 4./JG 77 when Operation Barbarossa began. From March 1942, when II./JG 5 was formed, he flew with the 4 *Staffel*. In August 1942 he took command of 6./JG 5 and was awarded the *Ritterkreuz* on 21 October 1942 for 41 aerial victories. In June 1943 he was appointed *Kommandeur* of III./JG 5 and on 2 August 1943 he received the *Eichenlaub* to the *Ritterkreuz* after gaining 112 kills. In May 1944 Ehrler was promoted to *Kommodore* of the entire JG 5. On 12 November 1944 the battleship *Tirpitz* was sunk by Lancasters and Ehrler was held responsible for the sinking. He was court-martialled and convicted to three years' imprisonment, but in February 1945 was instead posted to the *Geschwaderstab* of JG 7, where he flew Me 262 jets. On 6 April 1945, after downing two B-17s, he went missing in action. His final score of kills stood at 204, all but four having been achieved with JG 5 and its predecessors.

### Leutnant Rudi Linz

Linz was born on 14 February 1917 in Ilmenau, Thüringen. From March 1942 he was a member of III./JG 5, flying with the 8 *Staffel*. In July 1944, when all *Gruppen* were expanded to four *Staffeln*, he assumed the command of 12./JG 5. On 9 February 1945 his Fw 190A-8 (Blue 4, WNr 732183) was shot down by Beaufighters and he was crushed to death. His tally then amounted to 70 kills and he received the *Ritterkreuz* posthumously in March 1945.

### Leutnant August Mors

Mors was born on 20 June 1921 in Sigmaringen, Württenberg. He joined 6./JG 5 in summer 1942 and in June 1944 was transferred to 1./JG 5 on the English Channel front. On 6 August 1944 his Bf 109G received hits from the return fire of heavy bombers; Mors bailed out, hitting trees, and died two days later. On 24 October 1944 he received the *Ritterkreuz* posthumously for 60 aerial victories, 12 of which were in the invasion area.

### Oberfeldwebel Rudolf Müller

Müller was born on 21 November 1920 in Frankfurt am Main. He flew with 6./JG 5 from March 1942, when the II *Gruppe* of JG 5 was formed. On 19 June 1942 he became the first JG 5 holder of the Rit-

terkreuz, having gained 41 kills. On 19 April 1943 his Bf 109G-2 (Yellow 3, WNr 14810) was shot down by 609 IAP Hurricanes. He made a forced landing and was captured, eventually disappearing during his imprisonment. His final score was 94, including five Hurricanes on 23 April 1942.

### Leutnant Jakob Norz

Norz was born on 20 October 1920 in Saulgrub, Oberbayern. In late 1942 he joined III./JG 5. He flew with the 8 *Staffel* and on 26 March 1944 received the *Ritterkreuz* for 70 aerial victories. In July 1944 his *Staffel* became 11./JG 5. On 16 September 1944 Norz's Bf 109G-6 (Yellow 8, WNr 412199) was shot down by 20 IAP Airacobras; he bailed out too low and was killed. His score stood then at 117, having scored the most in one day – 12 – on 27 June 1944.

### Oberleutnant Walter Schuck

Schuck was born on 30 July 1920 in Frankenholz in Saar. From 1941 he flew with II./JG 77 in Norway, and from March 1942 with III./JG 5. On 8 April 1944 he received the *Ritterkreuz* after 84 aerial victories. Next month he became *Staffelkapitän* of 7./JG 5 and in July 1944 this unit became 10./JG 5. On 30 September 1944 Schluck was awarded the *Eichenlaub* to the *Ritterkreuz* for 171 kills. In February 1945 he was posted to JG 7 to fly the Me 262, and in March became the last *Staffelkapitän* of 3./JG 7. He claimed 198 kills with JG 5 and a further eight with the jets. On 17 June 1944 he scored twelve kills.

### Major Theodor Weissenberger

Weissenberger was born on 21 December 1914 in Mühlheim in Main. In September 1941 he was attached to 1.(Z)/JG 77 as a heavy-fighter pilot. After 23 victories with Bf 110 he was posted to 6./JG 5 in September 1942 and was awarded the *Ritterkreuz* on 13 November 1942 for 38 kills. In June 1943 he took over the command of 7./JG 5 and received the *Eichenlaub* to the *Ritterkreuz* on 2 August 1943, after 112 kills. In September he was posted to lead 6./JG 5 and became *Kommandeur* of II./JG 5 in March 1944 after Carganico. From June 1944 onwards he was *Kommandeur* of I./JG 5, again after Carganico, at the Allied invasion front, gaining 25 kills in less than three weeks. In November 1944 he became *Kommandeur* of I./JG 7 flying Me 262 jets and from January 1945 became *Kommodore* of JG 7 for the remainder of the war. After 200 kills with JG 5 and its predecessors, he attained a further eight using the jets. On 7 July 1943 he made seven kills in one sortie – the greatest number he achieved in one day. On 10 June 1950 he was killed in a car race at Nürnburgring.

**Right:** On 19 June 1942 *Feldwebel* Rudolf Müller was awarded the *Ritterkreutz* (Knight's Cross). He was the first member of JG 5 to be so honoured while flying with 6 *Staffel* as part of II *Gruppe*. For this occasion *Luftflotte* 5 commander *General Oberst* Hans-Jürgen Stumpff (facing the camera) arrived at Petsamo, at the time located by the Arctic Sea in northern Finland. *Luftflotte* 5 was in charge of aerial operations over Scandinavia and northern Finland. (via P. Petrick)

**Right:** *Feldwebel* Rudolf Müller after receiving the *Ritterkreuz* (worn round his neck). He won the decoration for achieving 41 confirmed aerial hits, while becoming the first of the great aces on the Arctic front. (via K. Maesel)

**Below:** *General Oberst* Stumpff inspects the personnel of JG 5, which are lined up for the medal-awarding ceremony. To his right is *Hauptmann* Horst Carganico, *Kommandeur* of II./JG 5, who while heading 1./JG 77 won the *Ritterkreuz*, on 25 September 1941. His score stood then at 27 victories. (via K. Maesel)

**Left:** *Oberleutnant* Theodor Weissenberger points to his 112 aerial victories. Awarded the *Ritterkreuz* 13 November 1942 for shooting down 38 Russian aircraft, he is shown here at Petsamo, as the *Staffelkapitän* of 7./JG 5, receiving the *Eichenlaub* (Oak Leaves) on 2 August 1943. (Bundesarchiv)

**Right:** Messerschmitt Bf 110F-2 heavy fighters in formation over Salmijärvi, northern Finland, during summer 1942. During the previous six months the *Zerstörerstaffel* had experienced three name changes, having been 13.(Z)/JG 5 since 26 June 1942. The foremost aircraft bears the code LN+SR; the letter R dates back to 7./ZG 76's two-year involvement in the occupation of Norway. (via P. Petrick)

**Opposite page, bottom:** Junkers Ju 88A-4 bomber serialled JK-273 of the Finnish Air Force. Twenty-four were bought from Germany in early 1943 and they all served with Lentolaivue 44. This particular machine was flown by 1st Lieutenant Tauno Iisalo, who as one of nineteen airmen received the highest military decoration of Finland, the Mannerhein Cross. JK-273 is parked under camouflage nets at Onttola air base in August 1943, just before the first major mission. (Pehr Schalin)

**Below:** 8./JG 5 leader *Oberleutnant* Hermann Segatz in front of his Bf 109E-7 at Helsinki Malmi airport in early 1942. The emblem under the cockpit is the Tirolean eagle, showing the pilot's origin. Segatz led his *Staffel* well into 1943 and went on to score at least 31 victories. (via B. Barbas)

**Left:** 2./KG 30 bomber 4D+CK was a Junkers Ju 88A-5, seen here at Kirkenes in Northern Norway in June 1942. The main unit, I./KG 30, was usually stationed at Banak and flew against the Allied PQ convoys in the Northern Atlantic and Arctic Ocean until July 1943. (via P. Petrick)

**Lower left:** The commander of *Luftflotte* 1, *General Oberst* Alfred Keller, on a formal visit to Helsinki Malmi, Finland, 11 August 1942. His Heinkel He 111 VIP transport is coded DL+OC. *Luftflotte* 1 operated south of the Gulf of Finland in charge of the Leningrad sector. (SA-kuva)

**Below:** The runway of Stavanger Sola airfield in central Norway proved to be too short for this Junkers Ju 52/3m transport aircraft. The occasion was the invasion of Norway on 9 April 1940. The cowling of the centre engine bears the tactical marking for this operation. (via K. Maesel)

**Above:** This Junkers Ju 52/3m transport, assigned to 2./KGr.z.b.V 172, is under outdoor engine overhaul at Stavanger Sola, spring 1940. A large invasion detachment flew to Sola as it was the main base at the North Sea, thus eliminating the possible arrival of British forces. (via K. Maesel)

**Below:** Close-up of the 2./KGr.z.b.V 172 emblem. On the 1 *Staffel* emblem the eight-pointed star was white, whereas on the 3 *Staffel* it was yellow. (via K.Maesel)

**Left:** These Ju 52/3m transports, which took part in the first phase of the invasion of Norway, were fitted with machine guns in the dorsal turret. Here a gunner of CF+IZ keeps watch. (via K. Maesel)

**Opposite page, top:** This Ju 52/3m (coded 1Z+HM), deployed by 4./KGr.z.b.V 1, is unloading troops and equipment on a recently built wooden planking, in a Norwegian airfield in summer 1940. The Berlin bear emblem can only just be seen on the nose. (via K. Maesel)

**Opposite page, bottom:** A Heinkel He 111H weather reconnaissance plane of *Westa* 5 at Banak in northern Norway during summer 1942. In the backgound is a Junkers Ju 52 transport, most certainly from KGr.z.b.V. 108, which was by far the largest operator of its kind in the north. (Author's collection)

**Below:** Spring 1940. German troops hoist a Ju 52/3m at Vaernes after the right wheel has run into a ditch. The invasion tactical sign is clearly indicated on the centre cowling. (via K. Maesel)

**Left:** An Arado Ar 196A-3 seaplane deployed by *Bordenfliegergruppe* 196. Three aircraft of this unit, T3+DH, T3+HH and T3+CK, were based at Santahamina near Helsinki on 6 June 1942. (Author's collection)

**Centre left:** An Ar 196A, still showing the *Stamm-kennzeichen.* This type saw limited use by both German and Finnish aircrews in guerrilla support missions over the eastern Karelian wilderness. During summer 1942, *Kurierkette* AOK Lappland used two Arados (from BFGr.196); the following summer the Finns flew a similar-looking GA+DO with Detachment Malinen. (Author's collection)

**Lower left:** *See-aufklärungsgruppe* 130 was formed on 10 July 1943 from elements of Kü.Fl.Gr. 406, 706 and 906, part of which had stayed in northern Norway since the onset of Operation Barbarossa. Its main equipment included Blohm und Voss Bv 138 seaplanes, flying mainly from Billefjord to look for allied convoys in the Northern Atlantic and the Arctic Sea. This example is from SAGr. 125, operating in the Black Sea (Author's collection)

**Above:** II./JG 77 was transferred to the island of Sylt for the invasion of Denmark and Norway. *Lt* Demes is shown having just returned from a sortie on 27 March 1940 in his Bf 109E-4 "White 11". Below the cockpit, from left, are the emblems of the II *Gruppe* and 4 *Staffel*. When JG 5 was formed two years later, this *Staffel* became 4./JG 5 in March 1942. (PK-Photo)

**Below:** Messerschmitt Bf 109E-4s of II./JG 77 at Oslo Fornebu airport, spring 1940. After the invasion of Norway the main part of this *Gruppe* returned to Germany. "Red 13" in the centre belonged to 5 *Staffel*. (via B.Hafsten)

**Opposite page, top:** The *Kommandeur* of III./JG 5, *Hptm.* Günter Scholz, flies his Bf 109E-7 over Petsamo in summer 1942. Below the wind screen is the *Gruppe* emblem, a flag of Finland with a Lapp boot. The yellow rudder carries his 30 victory bars. The yellow cowling underside was a standard German identification marking. (Bundesarchiv)

**Opposite page, bottom:** A Bf 109E of I./JG 77, Rovaniemi, summer 1941. This aircraft is an E-3 upgraded to E-7 standards. The lower wing tips are painted yellow to denote the eastern front. The yellow spinner tip would also indicate that the machine belonged to the 3 *Staffel*. (via B. Barbas)

**Above:** A Bf 109E-7 of 7./JG 5, Herdla near Bergen, spring 1942. This *Staffel* was founded in November 1941 and became part of the III Gruppe, which was formed at Trondheim during February–March 1942. 7./JG 5 flew in April 1942 to Petsamo, where it was joined by the 8 *Staffel* in May and 9 *Staffel* in July. The 7 *Staffel* badge is just below the windscreen. (via B. Olsen)

**Below:** "White 8" was a Bf 109E-7 assigned to 7./JG 5 and flown by a future ace, *Fw.* Franz Dörr. It is shown here at Bodö in March 1942 with the yellow eastern front band, but lacking the III Gruppe marking, which was typical during the early career of the unit. (via B. Barbas)

**Above:** Bf 109F-4 with *Stammkennzeichen* VE+TU at Helsinki Malmi airport, from where it left for Pori on 23 May 1942 and went on to JG 5 in northern Finland. Pori had a *Feldflugpark* (forward aircraft pool) – a depot from where the Germans dispatched aircraft to the north and carried out major overhauls. (E. Emaus)

**Top left and below left:** Messerschmitt Bf 109 and Bf 110 fighters assembled at Kauhava in western Finland, 29 October 1941. These aircraft are on the way to the north – to JGr.z.b.V, which was the predecessor of II./JG 5. The aircraft in the foreground, Bf 109E-3 (NG+QP), has a full yellow engine cowling, while the other Bf 109E-7s have the usual yellow cowling undersides. (Finnish Air Force)

**Below:** Another Bf 109F-4 at Helsinki Malmi airport. On 23 April 1942 CI+MM, *Werke Nummer* 10173, flew to Pori on its way to JG 5. There is speculation about the camouflage colours of these JG 5 machines; it is believed that these newly-built Erla machines were in the standard 74/75/76 grey scheme with the splinter pattern further down the fuselage. (E. Emaus)

**Above:** Future high-ranking ace and fighter leader *Leutnant* Heinrich Ehrler poses in front of a 4./JG 5 Bf 109F-4 at Petsamo in summer 1942. Many early Messerschmitts in the north like this one had bright yellow wing tips as a quick identification marking. (PK-Photo)

**Below:** The adjutant of III./JG 5, *Oblt.* Rudolf Lüder, takes off in a Bf 109F-4 from Petsamo in summer 1942. This *Gruppe* was usually the last to convert to new fighter versions. It was not until August 1942 that the Bf 109F-4 fully replaced the Bf 109E-7. Similar development was also seen with later Bf 109G subtypes. (Bundesarchiv)

**Above:** A Bf 109F-4 "Yellow 4" of 9./JG 5 seen over the Petsamo area in summer 1942. The first F models were attached to the III. *Gruppe* in March 1942 and stayed there for two years. (via P. Petrick)

**Below:** "White 6" of 7./JG 5 being prepared for a mission at Petsamo in summer 1942. Both the lower cowling and wing tips of this Bf 109F-4 have received a coat of fresh yellow paint. (Bundesarchiv)

**Above:** *Fw.* Jakob Norz of 8./JG 5 in front of his Bf 109G-2 "Black 8" in summer 1943. On 26 March 1944 he was decorated with the Knight's Cross and eventually scored 117 aerial victories by the time of his death in action on16 September 1944. (via B. Barbas)

**Left:** *Fw.* Rudolf Müller of 6./JG 5 receives a wreath made of pine twigs after scoring II./JG 5's 500th aerial victory. The baton he holds is notched with each of his personal victories. He is pictured dismounting from his Bf 109F-4 at Petsamo in June 1942. (PK-Photo)

**Above:** *Fw.* Heinrich Bartels of 8./JG 5 (behind the wreath) after returning from his 100th mission, Petsamo, 11 September 1942. Two months later Bartels received the Knight's Cross and later flew with IV./JG 27, claiming a total of 99 victories. His Bf 109F-4 "Black 13" displays both III. *Gruppe* and 8 *Staffel* badges, and his wife's name. (via P. Petrick)

**Right:** 6./JG 5 pilots *Fw.* Hans Döbrich (pictured left; 65 victories and Knight's Cross on 19 September 1943) and *Ofw.* Albert Brunner (53 victories and Knight's Cross on 3 July 1943) at Alakurtti in spring 1943. Behind is a Bf 109G-2/R6 "Yellow 10" flown by Döbrich. On the nose is the 6 *Staffel* badge. (via B. Barbas)

**Opposite page, top:** "Black 15" was a Bf 109F-4 assigned to 8./JG 5, seen here at Petsamo in autumn 1943. *Fw.* Rudolf Mayer is pictured between two mechanics. At this stage the III. *Gruppe* marked the machines with a disc, which can be seen behind the cross on the fuselage. This was usually connected with the IV. *Gruppe* of a *Geschwader.* (via B. Barbas).

**Left:** Bf 109F-4 of 8./JG 5, Petsamo, spring 1943. Believed to be flown by the *Staffelkapitän Hptm.* Hermann Segatz, who scored at least 31 aerial victories with the unit. (via B. Barbas)

**Above:** A Bf 109G-2 of III./JG 5 at Petsamo in summer 1943. This fighter type began its assignment to the unit in April 1943 and remained in the inventory for more than a year. "Yellow 10" of the 9 *Staffel* has freshly painted wing tips. (via P. Petrick)

**Below:** "Black 10" was a Bf 109F-4 of 8./JG 5, seen here at Petsamo in summer 1942. The identification markings on the wing tips are clearly shown. (via P. Petrick)

**Opposite page, top:** Two Bf 109F-4s of 7./JG 54 arriving at Utti, 23 June 1942. "White 1" was flown by the *Staffelkapitän Oblt.* Friedrich Rupp, who was decorated with the Knight's Cross on 24 January 1943, having achieved 52 aerial victories. (O. Könönen)

**Opposite page, bottom:** Bf 109G-2s assigned to II./JG 54 used Helsinki Malmi base in April 1943 during missions to cover the steel anti-submarine net deployed across the Gulf of Finland. "Black 1" was usually flown by the 5 *Staffel* leader. (O. Marttila)

**Above:** II./JG 5s returned to Alakurtti in early March 1944, for two months. "Black 4" was flown by 208-victory ace *Hptm.* Theodor Weissenberger, who became the *Gruppen Kommandeur* in Finland on 27 March 1944. Note the temporary winter camouflage adorning the plane. (via P. Petrick)

**Below:** A Bf 109F-4 assigned to 6./JG 5 at Petsamo in November 1942. "Yellow 1" was usually flown by *Fw.* Walter Schuck, who went on to score 206 aerial victories. A hot-air trunk is being used to warm up the engine. (H. Schmidt)

**Above:** *Hptm.* Horst Carganicos's famous Micky Mouse machine, an early Bf 109G-6, at Alakurtti in September 1943. Carganico remained in command of II./JG 5 until 27 March 1944. He was killed in combat two months later leading the I. *Gruppe.* (Bundesarchiv)

**Left:** Knight's Cross holder and III./JG 5 *Kommandeur* Franz Dörr sits on the cockpit sill of his Bf 109G-6 at Petsamo in summer 1944. Oddly, his collar patches still show the rank of an *Oberleutnant* despite his being listed as a *Hauptmann* on receiving the *Ritterkreuz*, which he is wearing here. Dörr was one the unit's top aces with 128 victories. (via B. Barbas)

**Above left:** *Hptm.* Heinrich Ehrler in front of his early model Bf 109G-6 at Alakurtti. "Yellow 12" (**also pictured below**), still wearing the 6./JG 5 colours, was among the first to arrive in the north. In June 1943 Ehrler was appointed to command III./JG 5. On 2 August he received the Oak Leaves (**above right**) to his Knight's Cross after achieving 112 aerial victories, which were appropriately marked on the rudder. (via B. Barbas and U. Larsstuvold)

**Above and left:** A Bf 109G-2 of Stab/III./JG 5, Petsamo, winter 1943/44. Four pilots amuse themselves with a sleigh drive. Obviously the cargo was too much for two reindeers as a third one was brought to the scene while the Messerschmitt prepares for take-off. (via P. Petrick)

**Above:** A Bf 109G-4 reconnaissance fighter of 1.(H)/32 at Alakurtti in March 1944. At this time the unit began conversion to single-seaters alongside the Focke Wulf Fw 189. (Bundesarchiv)

**Below:** When the Soviet longe-range bomber command ADD began night bombing of Helsinki and other cities on 5–6 February 1944, a week later twelve I./JG 302 night fighters arrived at Malmi for three months. A Bf 109G-6 "Red 29" warms up prior to take-off at Malmi on 28 February 1944. During two night raids the 109s shot down six Soviet aircraft. (SA-kuva)

**Opposite page, top:** II./JG 54 *Kommendeur Maj.* Erich Rudorffer's Fw 190A-6 at Immola in late June 1944. Rudorffer headed the fighter element of *Gefechtsverband Kuhlmey* which included 4 and 5 *Staffeln*. On 25 January 1945 Rudorffer won the Swords to his Knight's Cross with Oak Leaves. By the end of the war he had won 222 victories. (C-E. Bruun)

**Opposite page, bottom:** "White 7" of 4./JG 54 during a stop at Käkisalmi on 18 June 1944. This Focke Wulf Fw 190A-6 picked up maps from the Brewster-equipped Finnish fighter squadron HLeLv 26 then stationed there. (C-E. Bruun)

**Above:** Fw 190A-6 of 5./JG 54 just before take-off at Immola on 2 July 1944. In the cockpit of "Black 1" is *Lt.* Gerhard Thyben, who managed to pull his fighter in the air a moment later, just when the Soviet air forces raided Immola and the rain of bombs began. Thyben finished the war with the Knight's Cross, awarded on 8 April 1945, and 157 aerial victories. (SA-kuva).

**Below:** "Black 2" of 5./JG 54 taxies into Immola in early July 1944. It was regularly piloted by *Oblt.* Helmut Radtke. During the six-week stay in Finland, Rudorffer's fighters shot down 126 aircraft. (P. Saari)

**Above:** A Fw 190A-3 of 1./JG 5 at Herdla Bergen in late 1942. The Focke Wulfs were in the inventory of I./JG 5 from June 1942 to July 1943. The *Gruppe* operated quite independently. The main HQ staff were with III. *Gruppe* in Northern Lappland operating against the Soviet forces, leaving I. *Gruppe* in Norway to guard that country's coastline against RAF raids from across the North Sea. (via P. Petrick)

**Below:** A Fw 190A-3 fighter bomber of 14.(Jabo)/JG 5 at take-off from Petsamo in summer 1943. This *Staffel* became operational in February 1943 and was mainly used against maritime targets in the Arctic Sea. In January 1944 it became 4./SG 5 and was renamed 1./SG 5 in May. It flew out of Finland for two months, part of it as a section of *Gefechtsverband* Kuhlmey. (via K. Maesel)

**Opposite page, top:** A Fw 190F-8 of 1./SG 5 at Immola, 28 June 1944. "Black 10" was usually piloted by *Fw.* Hartmut Gettwart. As part of *Gefechtsverband* Kuhlmey, this *Staffel* was mainly used in precision bombing of bridges and similar demanding targets. (SA-kuva)

**Opposite page, bottom:** A Fw 190F-8, coded Q9+AB, Werke Nummer 931666, of I./SG 5 *Kommandeur Maj.* Fritz Schröter, Utti, 7 August 1944. Schröter had won the Knight's Cross on 24 September 1942 for harassing British shipping in the English Channel. His *Gruppe* stayed in Utti for ten days only and left for Estonia on 13 August 1944. (Author's collection)

**Left:** Messerschmitt Bf 110E-2 with *Stammkennzeichen* VN+CV at Kauhava on 29 October 1941. (The factory-applied a four-letter code that was effectively the aircraft's registration.) It is on its way to the north to join 1.(Z)/JG 77, the heavy fighter *Staffel* in *Luftflotte* (air fleet) 5. Through a couple of changes in the unit's designation, the *Staffel* became 13.(Z)/JG 5 in June 1942. (Finnish Air Force)

**Opposite Page, bottom:** A Bf 110C-4 heavy fighter, coded LN+DR of *Jagdgruppe* Stavanger, seen at Mandal in southern Norway in spring 1941. This machine had previously served with III./ZG 26, whose emblem is still on the nose. (via P. Petrick)

**Above:** II./ZG 76 *Kommandeur Maj.* Erich Groth (centre) in front of his Bf 110E-1 at Pori on 8 August 1941. Groth crashed to his death near Stavanger, Norway four days later in this M8+KC, *Werke Nummer* 6863. He had won the Knight's Cross on 1 October 1940 and scored 13 victories. (Author's collection)

**Below:** A Bf 110E-2 coded M8+YE, *Werke Nummer* 3761, of Stab/ZG 76 at Pori in summer 1941. It was flown by the *Zerstörer Staffel* leader, *Hptm.* Gerhard Schaschke, who was shot down in this machine on 4 August 1941 near Murmansk. He had scored at least 21 victories by then. (Author's collection)

**Above:** *Lt.* Felix Brandis force-landed his Bf 110E-1 LN+FR, *Werke Nummer* 4114, at Pajala, Sweden on 1 September 1941, and escaped being interned. He was the successor to Schaschke as the *Zerstörer Staffel* leader, but crashed to his death on 2 February 1942. (B. Widfeldt)

**Below:** *Oblt.* Felix Brandis also flew this Bf 110E-2, LN+LR, *Werke Nummer* 3759, seen at Helsinki Malmi in January 1942. At this point the heavy fighter *Staffel* was designated 6.(Z)/JG 5. Brandis had 14 victories to his credit. (Author's collection)

**Opposite page, top:** A Bf 110E-2 of 13.(Z)/JG 5 over the fjords of the Arctic Sea in summer 1942. The unit code was LN+KR; while the first part indicated the *Geschwader*, K was the individual letter and R usually denoted the 7 *Staffel*, but here it is marked as the *Zerstörer*. This was one of the few instances where an operational unit used two letters rather than an alpha-numeric combination for identity. (via T. Willis)

**Opposite page, below:** A Messerschmitt Bf 110F-2, coded LN+MR of 13.(Z)/JG 5, Pori, summer 1943. The *Staffel* emblem on the nose was derived from the three *Dachshund* pets kept by *Oblt.* Brandis. (Author's collection)

**Above:** A Junkers Ju 87R-2, coded A5+BH, of I./St.G 1 pictured on the Jonsvattnet ice, near Trondheim in April 1940. The "White B" and spinner tip indicated that this dive-bomber belonged to the *Staffel*. A SC 500 bomb rests on the hoist on its way to the fuselage bomb rack. (Bundesarchiv)

**Below:** A IV.(St)/LG 1 Stuka is being re-fuelled at Banak in northern Norway in spring 1941. This *Gruppe* of *Lehgeschwader* 1 was the only dive-bomber element of *Luftflotte* 5 operating to the east. The Ju 87B-2, coded L1+LU, belonged to the 10 *Staffel*. On the engine cover is the Gruppe emblem. (Bundesarchiv)

**Below:** An I./St.G 5 Ju 87B-2 parked on a forward base at Kiestinki in early 1942. Empty bomb racks would indicate a return from a mission to the Murkansk railway, a typical Stuka target at this period. IV.(St)/LG 1 was renamed I./St.G 5 in January 1942. (Finnish War Museum)

**Above:** A Ju 87B-2 of 2./St.G 5 being refuelled at Alakurtti in spring 1942. The old unit designation L1 can still be distinguished on the rear fuselage. The SC 50 bombs in the wing racks were fitted with extended fuses and used against troops and columns. (Author's collection)

**Above:** A Ju 87R-2 with *Stammkennzeichen* KC+YV on a transfer flight at Helsinki Malmi airport. It continued its journey on 11 January 1943 to Pori, on the way to St.G 5. The white distemper was roughly applied with a wide brush. (A. Korhonen)

**Below:** I./St.G 5 was renamed in October 1943 as I./SG 5, and in early December 1944 the unit flew to Idriza, Latvia as part of *Luftflotte* 1. Here a Ju 87D-5, coded L1+CB, of Stab/I./SG 5 takes off soon after the transfer to Latvia. (Bundesarchiv)

**Above:** 1./SG 3 *Staffelkapitän Oblt.* Hans Töpfer taxies a Ju 87D-5, coded S7+AH, into Immola on 2 July 1944. On 20 July 1944 Töpfer was decorated with the Knight's Cross while still in Finland. His and also other *Staffel* leaders' machines carried a small chevron in *Staffel* colours at the front of the fuselage code. (SA-kuva)

**Below:** A Ju 87D-5, coded S7+JH, after its return to Immola from a mission to the Karelian Isthmus on 2 July 1944. This machine was often flown by *Fw.* Oswald Godo. The *Geschwader* code S7 was painted in small characters just ahead of the yellow fuselage band. (SA-kuva).

**Above:** A Junkers Ju 88D-1 long-range reconnaissance aircraft, G2+IH of 1.(F)/124, pictured over the Arctic Sea in summer 1943. Different versions of Ju 88 equipped the unit throughout the campaign against Russia. Until September 1944 the main base was at Kirkenes. The *Staffel* emblem is on the nose. (via P. Petrick)

**Below:** A Ju 88A-6, coded M7+GH, of 1./KGr. 806 photographed outside the hangar at Utti on 11 July 1941. Early in Operation Barbarossa this unit was laying mines around the naval base of Kronstadt just outside Leningrad. (Finnish Air Force)

**Above:** This M7+AH was another Ju 88A-6 of 1./KGr. 806. It is shown parked at Helsinki Malmi airport after the first heavy snowfalls in late October 1941. The stubs on the nose and wingtips were the attachment points for balloon-cable fenders. (E.Laiho)

**Below:** A Ju 88D-1 recce plane G2+EH of 1.(F)/124 at Alakurtti in August 1943. Missions from here were extended to the Archangelsk-Moscow railway. The *Kette* Lappland emblem has been kept (on the nose). (PK-Photo)

**Above:** Junkers Ju 88A-4 bombers of 2./KG 30 flying over Banak in northern Norway during June 1943. Next month the I. *Gruppe* left the northern theatre as the last bomber outfit. Closest to camera is 4D+HK. (PK-Photo)

**Below:** A Ju 88A-5 of II./KG 30 warming up at Banak in August 1941. White unit designation indicates that this machine was mainly used in reconnaissance missions,

often over the Northern Atlantic to search for Allied convoys. (PK-Photo)

**Opposite page, top and bottom:** A Ju 88A-4, coded 4D+CP, of 6./KG 30 being refuelled at Nurmoila on the Olonets Isthmus in autumn 1942. Between September and November *Lt.* Peter Stahl flew several guerrilla support missions from here carrying food, ammunition and other equipment to patrols far behind the Russian lines. (P. Saari)

**Left:** A bomber crew stands in front of a Ju 88A-4 of I./KG 30 at Banak in December 1942. The I. *Gruppe* remained in the north in case the Allies resumed their convoys of aid and supplies to the USSR, which had temporarily been suspended. All other bomber units were flown urgently to the Mediterranean area, where Operation Torch put the Allies behind the German lines. (Bundesarchiv)

**Opposite page, top and bottom:** A Junkers Ju 188F-1 long-range reconnaissance plane of 3.(F)/Aufkl.Gr. 22 over the Leningrad sector in spring 1944. 4N+FL wears a suitable winter camouflage. This unit also flew in support of *Gefechtsverband* Kuhlmey during the following summer. (K. Karhila)

**Below:** A Ju 88A-5 coded 4D+LP, *Werke Nummer* 4376, of 6./KG 30 at Pori in summer 1941. The *Adler* (Eagle) *Geschwader* emblem is clearly shown. I. Gruppe, II. Gruppe, and III. Gruppe had red, white, and yellow backgrounds respectively. (P. Nurminen)

**Above:** A Dornier Do 17P long-range reconnaissance plane at Vaasa in western Finland during August 1941. Though this machine still wears the *Stammkennzeichen* BX+NK, it is believed that it served with 4.(F)/Aufkl.Gr. 11, which operated in the north for a time. (O. Kuuluvainen)

**Below:** A high-command Dornier Do 215B-1 of Aufkl.Gr.(F) Ob.d.L, coded T5+AC, paying a visit to Utti on 11 July 1941. On both upper and lower wing surfaces are the remains of the German civil registration. (Finnish Air Force)

**Above:** A Dornier Do 17Z of *Luftflotte* 1's communications flight, parked at Suulajärvi on the Karelian Isthmus, 15 June 1942. The aircraft coded U5+FA had belonged to Stab/KG 2, but now has on its tail the black-and-white 'chequerboard' symbol associated with *Luftflotte* (air fleet) planes. The aircraft was probably being used by an air fleet commander as a transport aircraft. (V. Lakio)

**Below:** A rarity at Helsinki Malmi airport in autumn 1941. This Dornier Do 217C-0 – one of only four built – was coded NF+UU, *Werke Nummer* 2710 and was most certainly used by Aufkl.Gr.(F) Ob.d.L. In addition to clandestine missions, it tested the suitability of new types. (Finnish Aviation Museum)

**Above:** A Dornier Do 17P reconnaissance machine of *Aufklärungskette* (F) Lappland at Rovaniemi in late October 1941, during an engine service with 1R+AH. In the northern theatre of war missions were flown with almost obsolete types. (Author's collection)

**Below:** A Dornier Do 17Z-3, coded 5K+CR, *Werke Nummer* 2818, parked at Tampere on 12 February 1942, when a Finnish Air Force Bristol Blenheim (furthest right; just visible by the Finnish swastika on the lower surface of the wing) smashed the nose of this and the next plane in passing. The 7./KG 3 unit had used this Dornier before it was deployed by Germany, with its neighbour, with the Finnish Air Force. (Finnish Air Force)

**Above:** A Do 17P revving up before a reconnaissance mission from Rovaniemi in winter 1941/42. 1R+AH was a member of *Aufklärungskette* (F) Lappland, whose insignia is portrayed on the nose. (Bundesarchiv)

**Below:** A Dornier Do 217J night fighter, coded N9+AA, on a visit to Alakurtti in March 1944. As an ex-night-fighter commander, the new head of *Luftflotte* 5, *Gen. Lt* Josef Kammhuber, used this as his hack, also revealed by the *Luftflotte* badge on the nose. This version of the badge has a red border and is superimposed with a Luftwaffe eagle to denote that it is a Commander-in-Chief's aircraft. (Bundesarchiv)

**Above:** This early Heinkel He 111E was stationed at Helsinki Malmi airport during the first half of May 1942 for ice reconnaissance over the western Gulf of Finland. Coded DB+LU, *Werke Nummer* 1293, the plane still bears the pre-war three-colour camouflage scheme. (A. Nieminen)

**Below:** The hack of *Luftflotte* 5 C-in-C, *Gen.Obst.* Hans-Jürgen Stumpff, was this Heinkel He 111H-6, coded N9+KA, *Werke Nummer* 4956. It is seen here on a visit to Tampere on 12

June 1943. The Luftflotte emblem can be seen above the swastika, oddly with the black-and-white fields reversed. (Author's collection)

**Opposite page, top and bottom:** This Heinkel He 111P-6, coded GA+OW, *Werke Nummer* 580, was a liaison aircraft for the staff of *Luftflotte* 1. On 27 June 1942 it stopped by at Nurmoila on the Olonets isthmus. The owl emblem on the nose remains unknown. (A. Bremer)

**Above and below:** The hack of Stab/SG 3 Heinkel He 111H-6, coded S7+FA, at Immola on 20 June 1944. The commander of *Gefechtsverband* Kuhlmey, *Obst.Lt.* Kurt Kulhmey, flew to Finland in this machine. He was also the *Kommodore* of SG 3 and had won the Knight's Cross on 15 July 1942. (C-E. Bruun)

**Opposite page, top:** A Heinkel He 111H-4 bomber of 1./KG 26, Pori, early 1942. The letter A in code 1H+AH usually

indicated that this machine was flown by the *Staffelkapitän*. (V. Ketonen)

**Opposite page, bottom:** A He 111H-4 torpedo-bomber, coded 1H+ML of 3./KG 26, at Helsinki Malmi airport in July 1942. It was piloted by the *Staffelkapitän, Hptm.* Fritz Luwer, who marked his ship sinkings with a silhouette on the rudder. (E. Lyly)

**Opposite page, top and bottom:** A Focke Wulf Fw 189A reconnaissance aircraft, parked at Helsinki Malmi airport. On 15 April 1943 with *Stammkennzeichen* RD+VM and RD+VK they departed to Pori on the way north to *Aufklärungsgruppe* 32. (E. Rinne)

**Below:** 1./Aufkl.Gr. 32 performed its 2000th mission on 24 July 1943, piloted by the *Staffelkapitän*, *Hptm.* Hoppe. It is celebrated here at Alakurtti with the appropriate wreath attached to the nose of the Fw 189A, which is coded V7+1F. Quite exceptionally, the digit 1 stood for the 1. *Staffel*, while the F was the individual letter. The *Staffelzeichen* (staff badge) is below the cockpit. (Bundesarchiv)

**Above:** This Fw 189A-3, Werke Nummer 0192, is on a visit to a not-so-distant Finnish base, Tiiksjärvi, in June 1943. V7+1J has a worn out camouflage; both engine cowlings are recent replacement items. (SA-kuva)

**Above and below:** On 10 August 1941, four Henschel Hs 126Bs landed at Vaasa in transit to Aufkl.Gr. 32. DE+AU still wears the emblem of 1.(H)/Aufkl.Gr. 13, while the others are just 'plain' close-range reconnaissance aircraft, DE+AZ, DL+FB and GD+NO. (U. Jaakkola)

**Opposite page, top:** A Hs 126B, coded V7+1C of 1.(H)/Aufkl.Gr. 32, parked at Alakurtti. On 20 December 1941 a propaganda unit arrived here to assess progress in the far north. The troops are using the only practical mode of transport for the snow. (Bundesarchiv)

**Opposite page, bottom:** Another V7+1C of 1.(H)/Aufkl.Gr. 32 shown leaving Finland from Helsinki Malmi airport, on 5 November 1942. Giving up the Henschels, this recce unit continued its work with the Fw 189As. (Finnish Aviation Museum)

**Opposite page, top:** A Fieseler Fi 156C-5 Storch, coded V7+1H, *Werke Nummer* 4487, of 1.(H)/Aufkl.Gr. 32 at Kemijärvi on 15 September 1941. Coincidentally, the *Staffel's* *Storch* (stork) emblem was painted on the nose. (SA-kuva)

**Opposite page, bottom:** A Fi 156C liaison aircraft, coded PP+XT, seen at Alakurtti in early winter of 1941/42. Random white paint has been sprayed onto the standard camouflage to make the plane fit better into the wintry terrain. Forward bases like Alakurtti were frequently subject to Russian air raids. (via U. Larsstuvold)

**Top right:** This Messerschmitt Bf 108 Taifun courier aircraft is with *Stammkennzeichen* VF+EC on a visit to Helsinki

Malmi in spring 1942. It is thought to have belonged to *Luftdienstkommando* (Air Service Command) Finnland. (K. Ritvanen)

**Above:** This French Caudron C.445 Goeland light passenger plane SK+XS was captured and pressed into use by the Luftwaffe. It is pictured here at Helsinki Malmi airport in July 1941. (Author's collection).

**Below:** Focke Wulf Fw 58C courier aircraft with the *Stammkennzeichen* TY+NR on a stop to Kauhava on 10 October 1941. The yellow eastern-front marking on the fuselage has been applied just below the cross. (Finnish Air Force)

**Above:** A Heinkel He 59D seaplane, coded PP+AO, at Kontiolahti in June 1943. It was leased from the Germans and this Finnish detachment, *Osasto* Malinen, used it for guerrilla transport and supply missions beyond the lines east of Lake Onega. (E. Jauri)

**Below:** When Adolf Hitler was flown to Finland on 4 June 1942 to congratulate the Finnish C-in-C, Marshall Garl Gustaf Emil Mannerheim, on his 75th birthday, BFGr. 196 transferred three Arado Ar 196As to Santahamina, near Helsinki, to secure the crossing of Hitler's Fw 200 over the Gulf of Finland. The machines were T3+CK, T3+DH and T3+GH. (Author's collection)

**Opposite page, top:** A Heinkel He 115C-1 seaplane, coded 8L+IH, of 1./Kü.Fl.Gr. 906, mooring at Santahamina. This machine was *Werke Nummer* 2729 and it was lost shortly afterwards in a Russian ambush east of Lake Onega, on 22 October 1942. (Finnish Air Force)

**Opposite page, below:** A Blohm und Voss Bv 138C-1 flying boat, coded +FL, of 3./SAGr. 130 at Billefjord quay, northern Norway, July 1943. This unit extended the maritime patrols way out into the North Atlantic. The unit badge on the nose dates back to Kü.Fl.Gr. 406. (PK-Photo)

**Above:** This Junkers Ju 52/3m transport aircraft of ex-KGr.z.b.V 40 is on a stop to Pori in early October 1941. The unit code 9P is from the previous owner. KGr.z.b.V 40 and 60 planes were *Gruppen*-activated for the airborne invasion of Crete in May 1941, after which they were disbanded. Many were subsequently taken into KGr.z.b.V 108, which became the major transport outfit in the *Luftflotte* 5 area. (U. Jaakkola)

**Below:** A Ju 53/3mg5e, coded 9P+EL, *Werke Nummer* 6950, of 3./KGr.z.b.V 108 at Kauhava, spring 1942. On 17 June 1942 this machine was badly damaged near Kauhava in a crash landing caused by engine trouble. (L. Piippo)

**Opposite page, top and bottom:** A Junkers Ju 52/3m, coded 1Z+IM, of 4./KGz.b.V 1 on a visit to Nurmoila, summer 1942. Many aircraft flying with *Luftflotte* 1 visited Nurmoila – the closest air base to the border – to the north of which the Finnish Air Force was in charge. (P. Saari and J. Sarasto)

**Left:** A suitably weathered Junkers Ju 52/3m, coded 4V+DR, of KGr.z.b.V 106 at Helsinki Malmi airport, summer 1941. On the nose is the Narvik shield carried by many planes from several units operating in the invasion of northern Norway. (Author's collection)

**Bottom left:** This Junkers Ju 52/3m transport, coded 9V+DD, of ex-KGr.z.b.V 60 is pictured at Kauhava on 29 September 1941. The machine ended up with KGr.z.b.V 108 and carries both the unit code and emblem of a previous owner. (Finnish Air Force)

**Above:** A Junkers Ju 52/3m, photographed from the control tower of Helsinki Malmi airport in summer 1941. The *Stammkennzeichen* was NO+IE. (Author's collection)

**Below:** Italian Savoia Marchetti S.81/AR, coded 8Q+CH, of 1./TGr. 10 at Immola, June 1944. This unit formed part of the transport element of *Gefechtsverband* Kuhlmey that carried non-flying personnel. Behind the cockpit is the flag of *Aeronautica Nazionale Repubblicana*. (C-E. Bruun)

**Above:** A Focke Wulf Fw 200C-3/U9, one of Hitler's travel machines and coded KE+IX, *Werke Nummer* 0099 at Helsinki Malmi airport on 26 June 1942. Marshall Mannerheim is shown arriving from Germany after his sole visit to Hitler and is about to exit the plane. (Author's collection)

**Below:** A Fw 200C-4/U1 VIP transport, coded CG+AE, of *Regierungsstaffel*, pictured at Helsinki Malmi airport, 27 June 1944. The new C-in-C of the 20. *Gebirgsarmee*, *Gen.Obst.* Lothar Rendulic, arrived in this aircraft and paid a courtesy visit to Marshall Mannerheim. (Bundesarchiv)